EARTHQUAKES

© Aladdin Books Ltd 2002

Designed and produced by
Aladdin Books Ltd
28 Percy Street
London W1T 2BZ

Revised and updated edition published in 2002
First published in Great Britain in 1992 by
Franklin Watts
96 Leonard Street
London EC2A 4XD

Design: David West
          Children's Book
          Design
Designer: Stephen Woosnam-Savage
Editors: Fiona Robertson
          Libby Volke
Picture Researchers: Emma Krikler
                      Brian Hunter Smart
Illustrator: Mike Saunders

ISBN 0 7496 4408 7 (hardcover)
ISBN 0 7496 4806 6 (paperback)
A CIP catalogue record for this book is available
from the British Library.

Printed in UAE

Natural Disasters

EARTHQUAKES

JANE WALKER

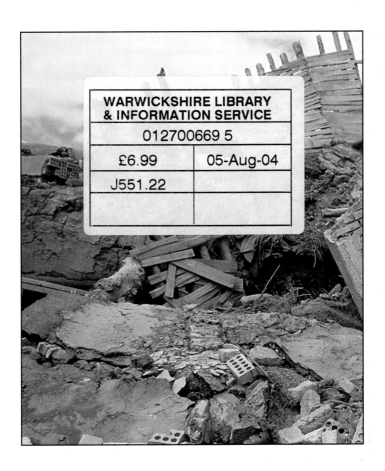

FRANKLIN WATTS
LONDON • SYDNEY

CONTENTS

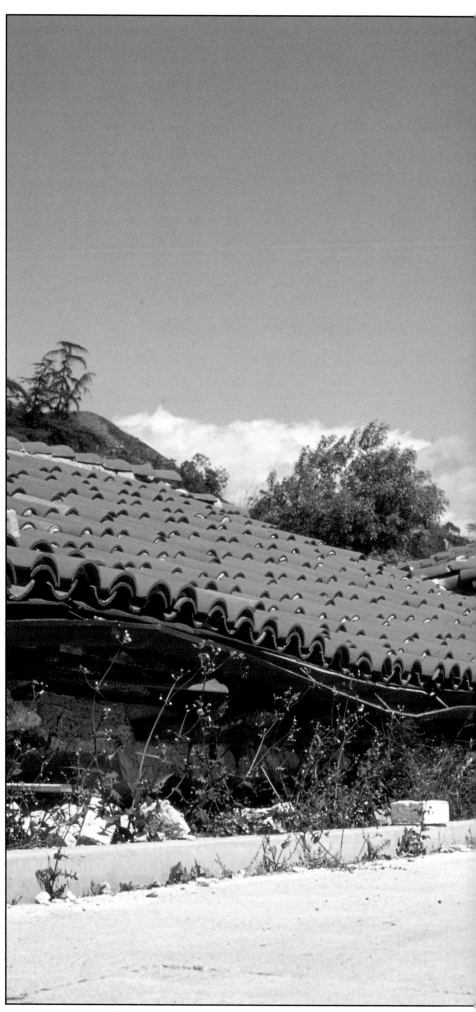

INTRODUCTION

The destructive power of an earthquake is one of the most deadly of all natural forces. In just a few seconds, these massive vibrations of the Earth's crust can shatter whole communities. The earthquakes unleashed on some of the world's most densely populated areas are not necessarily the largest. Yet they cause the greatest amount of damage and the highest number of deaths. Scientists hope to avoid such devastating losses by developing more accurate methods of earthquake prediction.

WHAT IS AN EARTHQUAKE?

An earthquake is the sudden, and often violent, trembling of part of the Earth's surface. It sends shock waves racing through the Earth's crust, which is the name given to the rocky outer layer surrounding the Earth. Earthquakes are generated in the huge tile-like sections, called plates, which make up this crust.

A plate boundary is the area where two of these plates meet. Continual movement at plate boundaries creates a build-up of pressure beneath the surface. Rocks are elastic up to a point and can absorb the strain from this pressure for hundreds, even thousands, of years. Eventually, however, they snap, or rupture, at their weakest point, relieving the enormous strain. Huge amounts of energy are released as shock waves, called seismic waves. These radiate outwards from the point where the rocks fractured. The area within the Earth's crust where the shock waves begin is called the earthquake's focus. The place on the surface directly above the focus is the epicentre.

In a subduction zone, new ocean floor is dragged back into the mantle. The resulting heat and strain cause deep-focus-earthquakes as far down as 645 km.

Subduction zone

At an oceanic ridge (see page 8), hot molten rock, called magma, rises and creates strain in the rocks until it is relieved by an earthquake. Earthquakes caused in this way are usually small.

Oceanic ridge

Deep-focus earthquake

Rising magma

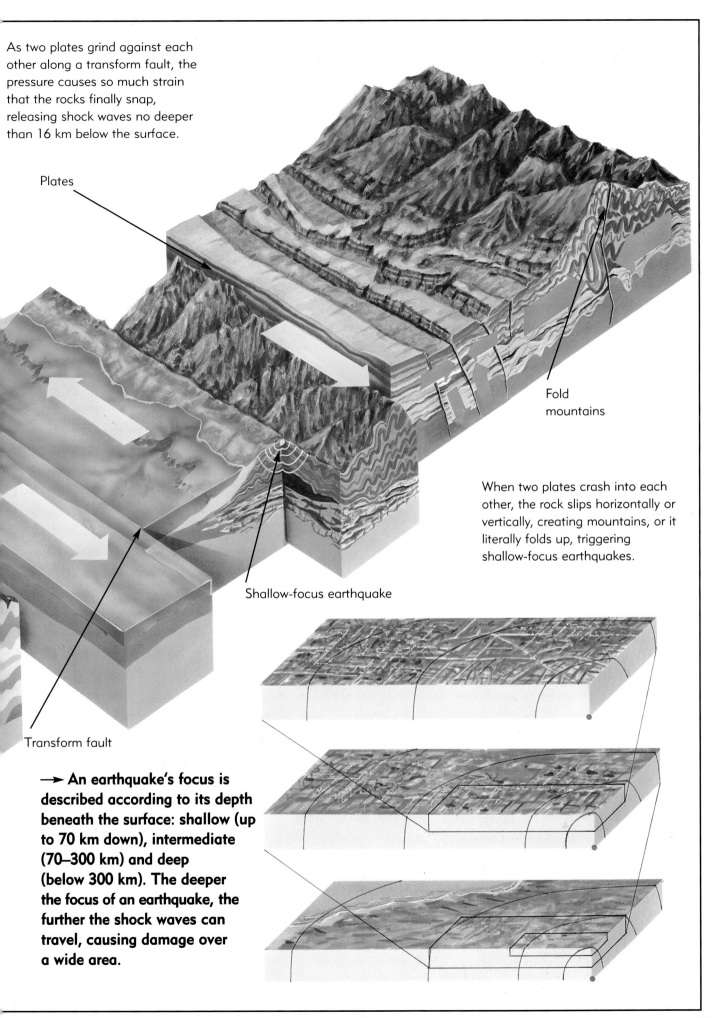

As two plates grind against each other along a transform fault, the pressure causes so much strain that the rocks finally snap, releasing shock waves no deeper than 16 km below the surface.

Plates

Fold mountains

When two plates crash into each other, the rock slips horizontally or vertically, creating mountains, or it literally folds up, triggering shallow-focus earthquakes.

Shallow-focus earthquake

Transform fault

→ **An earthquake's focus is described according to its depth beneath the surface: shallow (up to 70 km down), intermediate (70–300 km) and deep (below 300 km). The deeper the focus of an earthquake, the further the shock waves can travel, causing damage over a wide area.**

THE MOVING EARTH

The Earth consists of three separate layers: the crust is made of giant plates which are constantly moving. The plates float in the hot molten rock, called magma, of the upper mantle. Pressure in the mantle forces the magma up through the crust along the oceanic ridges. These areas are known as constructive plate margins because when the magma cools and hardens, it forms new ocean floor.

In subduction zones, or destructive plate margins, ocean floor is destroyed when plates collide and the edge of one plate is dragged down into the mantle. At a third type of boundary, the transform fault, plates are simply sliding past each other, and so the fault is neither a constructive nor a destructive boundary. Plate movements at all three types of boundary can give rise to earthquakes.

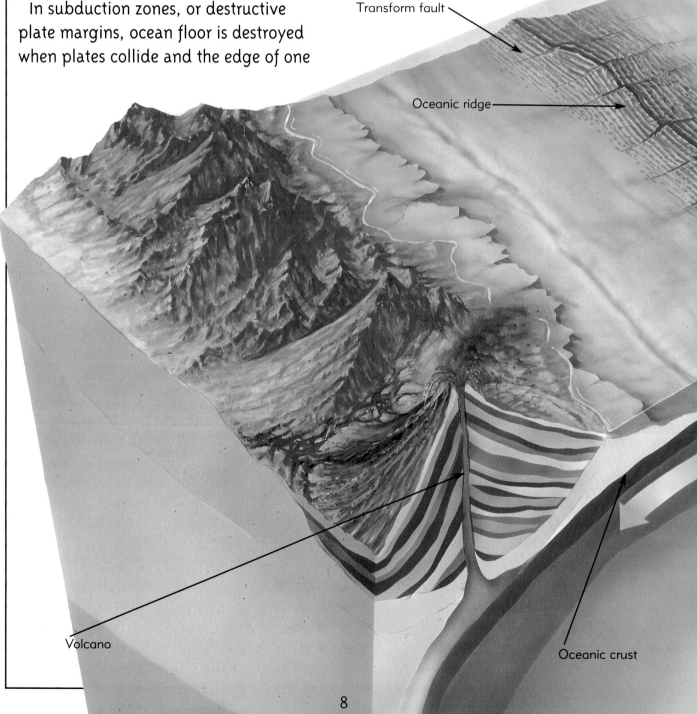

Transform fault

Oceanic ridge

Volcano

Oceanic crust

Oceanic trench

Subduction
zone

Continental
crust

The rocky crust, or lithosphere, which surrounds the Earth can be quite thin in places. The oceanic crust, which is made of basalt, has an average thickness of 7 km. The continental crust, which makes up the land areas, is 35–40 km thick, and consists mostly of granite.

Molten
magma

➤ This map shows the different plates of the Earth's crust. Most earthquakes occur in narrow zones that coincide with the plate boundaries.

— Plate boundaries
▓ Earthquake zones

9

AN EARTHQUAKE BEGINS

In the period before an earthquake, the pressure building up in the rock layers beneath the ground causes so much strain that cracks appear in walls and pavements. When the rocks finally snap, the first seismic waves to be released from the earthquake's focus are known as body waves. Body waves travel through the Earth and are of two types: primary (P) and secondary (S) waves. Waves that only travel along the surface of the Earth are surface, or long (L), waves.

Primary waves travel through solid rock, volcanic lava, water and even air at speeds of up to 8 km per second. P waves are followed by S waves, which travel more slowly, at about 6 km per second. When the body waves reach the surface, some are transformed into surface waves. Surface waves produce the most severe ground movements. A violent jolt is felt at the epicentre as the ground moves. The first tremor may last for only 30 to 60 seconds, but further tremors, or aftershocks, occur soon after as the disturbed rocks settle into a new position.

P waves are the first to be recorded at seismic monitoring stations. They squeeze and stretch the rocks as they pass through the Earth.

S waves shake the rocks up and down and from side to side. Unlike P waves, S waves cannot travel through fluids. This creates areas on the surface where there are no S waves.

Telltale signs

Certain warning signs have been noticed before an earthquake. Minor tremors make the Earth shake gently. As the rocks beneath begin to warp and bulge, swellings appear on the surface. They cause the ground to crack and finally burst open (shown right). Scientists in China have noticed that water in ponds and canals gives off strange smells, possibly due to gas building up underground.

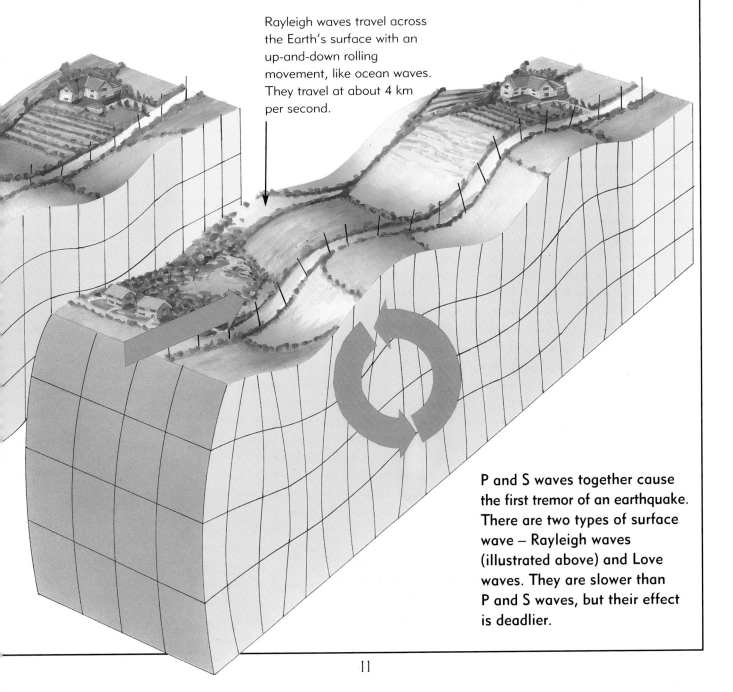

Rayleigh waves travel across the Earth's surface with an up-and-down rolling movement, like ocean waves. They travel at about 4 km per second.

P and S waves together cause the first tremor of an earthquake. There are two types of surface wave – Rayleigh waves (illustrated above) and Love waves. They are slower than P and S waves, but their effect is deadlier.

DEATH AND DESTRUCTION

As the roar and violent motion of a major earthquake are heard and felt, tall apartment buildings and office blocks often collapse in vast piles of rubble, burying hundreds of people. In Mexico City in 1985, the main tower of the Benito Juarez Hospital collapsed floor by floor, killing 1,000 patients and staff. Huge cracks appear as roads and pavements are ripped apart, and road and rail links to the stricken area are cut off, making it difficult for rescue workers to bring help. There is also a serious risk of fire from damaged electricity cables and gas pipes.

Earthquakes bring with them other deadly after-effects. Those that occur under the sea create giant waves, called *tsunamis*, which sweep in from the sea and lash the coast. The 1964 Alaskan quake created a *tsunami*, 21 m high in places, which raced towards Hawaii at over 645 km/h. Strong tremors caused nearby rivers to overflow, and dams and reservoirs to burst, triggering huge landslides. An earthquake in Peru in 1971 caused a massive chunk of ice to break off Mt Huascarán in the Andes Mountains. As the ice melted, it turned into an 80-m-high mudflow, which swept through the town of Yungay, killing 50,000 people.

Before and after

Mexico City (below) is built on layers of mud, clay, gravel and sand of a dried-up lake bed. Soil levels and buildings there can subside by up to 15 cm a year. Cities built on soft surfaces suffer most earthquake damage because the soft soil increases the effects of the seismic waves. Amazingly, the 52-storey headquarters of Mexico's state oil company, the tallest tower in Latin America, survived the shock waves of the 1985 earthquake. With the aid of special equipment, several dozen babies were rescued alive from the ruins of the city's hospitals.

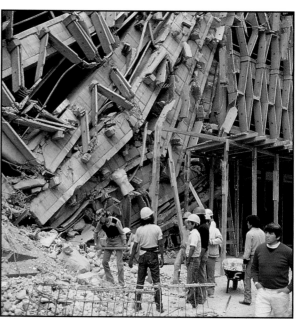

→ In January 1999, a 6.2-magnitude earthquake rattled Western Colombia, killing 1,200 people. Of the more than 20 towns affected, Armenia, shown right, was worst hit.

↓ A 7.2 magnitude quake struck Kobe, Japan, in January 1995. Lasting 20 seconds, it killed 6,430 people and was the most expensive natural disaster ever, causing record losses of £63.7 billion.

MEASURING EARTHQUAKES

The scientists who study the seismic waves released from the focus of an earthquake are called seismologists. Special measuring instruments, called seismographs, record the pattern of these seismic waves. Seismologists use these patterns to determine the strength and duration of an earthquake, as well as the amount of movement along a fault line. Taking readings at several different points on the Earth's surface also helps them to pinpoint the exact location of the earthquake's focus.

Two different scales are used to measure the strength of an earthquake. The most common one is the Richter Scale, devised by an American seismologist, Charles Richter, in 1935. It calculates the magnitude of an earthquake from seismograph recordings that measure the amount of energy released. An increase of 1 point on the Richter Scale means that an earthquake is ten times stronger than one with the next value below. An earthquake measuring less than 5 on the Richter Scale causes minimal damage, while a major earthquake measures 7 or more. The second scale is the Mercalli Scale, which calculates the intensity of an earthquake by assessing the damage it causes.

I: Felt by only a very few people. II: Felt by a few, on upper floors.

III: Similar to a passing vehicle.
IV: Felt by many people indoors.

V: Buildings tremble and trees shake.
VI: Felt by all. Plaster cracks.

VII: Bricks loosen. Difficult to stand. VIII: Damage to weak structures.

→ A scientist traces the marks made by a seismograph as it records the movements of the ground during an earthquake. Scientists can distinguish between the primary, secondary and surface waves.

IX: Pipes crack. Buildings collapse. X: Huge ground cracks. Landslides.

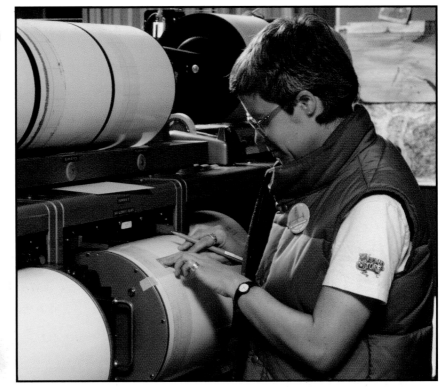

←The Mercalli Scale was invented in 1902 by an Italian seismologist, Giuseppe Mercalli, and modified during the 1930s by American scientists. The scale describes effects that range from tiny swaying movements (I) to total devastation (XII).

XI: Most buildings destroyed. *Tsunamis.* XII: Total destruction. Surface waves seen.

Seismographs

One type of seismograph records the horizontal movements of the Earth, and the other type records the vertical movements. A weight is attached to a frame by a sensitive spring. As the ground trembles, the weight remains stationary but the frame moves and a pen records the movement on paper wrapped around a rotating drum. This recording is called a seismogram.

EARTHQUAKES IN HISTORY

Many of the myths and legends surrounding earthquakes date back thousands of years. Some of the world's greatest civilizations have been built up around major earthquake zones such as China, the mountainous areas of the Middle East, Mexico and the lands around the Mediterranean Sea and India.

Ancient cultures believed that earthquakes were caused by the actions of huge beasts. Hindu mythology claimed that the Earth was supported by eight huge elephants. When one of the elephants became tired and lowered and shook its head, this resulted in an earthquake. According to Japanese legend, earthquakes are caused by the *namazu*, a giant catfish living in the mud beneath the Earth's surface. The *namazu* is something of a prankster who can only be controlled by the Kashima god. In October 1855, when the gods were said to be visiting a distant shrine, an earthquake struck the city of Edo (modern Tokyo). In the absence of the Kashima god, the catfish had hurled itself around and unleashed the earthquake.

↓ The Japanese legend of the *namazu* was depicted in many popular 19th-century prints. The one below shows the people of Edo attacking the *namazu* for unleashing the earthquake.

16

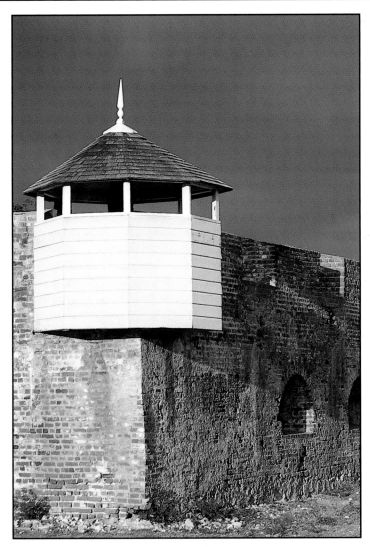

The first earthquake sensor

This instrument was designed by the Chinese in the 2nd century AD. During a tremor, a swinging weight opened the mouth of one of eight dragons. A small bronze ball dropped from the dragon's mouth onto the open-mouthed frog below, making a loud clang. The dragon with the empty mouth indicated the direction of the earthquake.

↑ The earthquake which devastated the Jamaican city of Port Royal (above) in 1692 left 2,000 people dead. Port Royal was an important pirate centre for the West Indies, trading in slaves and rum. Many people believed the earthquake was a punishment from God.

→ This engraving shows one of the effects of the earthquake which struck the Calabria region of southern Italy in 1783. About 50,000 people died in a series of earthquakes over a 7-week period. Later, the Academy of Sciences and Fine Letters in Naples set up a commission to assess the damage.

THE LISBON EARTHQUAKE

On the morning of All Saints' Day, 1 November 1755, in the city of Lisbon, capital of the Portuguese empire, many of the city's inhabitants were in church. At 9.40 am, everything began to shudder violently as the first shock waves of an earthquake reached the city. Buildings rocked from side to side, and the spires of the city's many churches swayed. In terror, worshippers in the cathedral of Santa Maria rushed out into the nearby square, only to be crushed to death as a second more violent tremor caused the cathedral to collapse, along with much of the rest of the city.

As the first tremors subsided, fire threatened to engulf the city as timber and furniture collapsed into fireplaces and set alight. A huge tsunami swept over the quaysides, sucking up people, masonry, ships and animals. About 60,000 people died in Lisbon that morning. Tremors were observed as far away as Sweden and Scotland, and in Spain and North Africa thousands more died as buildings collapsed. Scientists have estimated that the quake would have measured 8.75 on the Richter Scale.

From the banks of the River Tagus, a huge 15-m wave hurled itself across the city.

The epicentre of the Lisbon earthquake was believed to be about 322 km southwest of the city. The earthquake occurred along a transform fault within the giant Eurasian Plate.

The shock waves from the first tremor travelled from the epicentre to Lisbon within seconds.

← Before its destruction in the 1755 earthquake, the city of Lisbon (inset left) was a great trading centre for silks, spices and paintings, and an important centre of Western thought and culture.

Fire spread throughout the city and burned for almost three days, destroying everything in its path.

→ After the earthquake of 1755, the low-lying *Baixa* district of Lisbon was rebuilt with straight, wide streets. The older parts of the city, situated on higher ground, escaped destruction by the *tsunami*.

THE SAN ANDREAS FAULT

The giant San Andreas Fault system stretches for more than 1,210 km along the coast of California in the United States. This transform fault lies along the boundary between the Pacific Plate and the North American Plate. As these two plates constantly grind against each other, some of the resulting strain is released from time to time by tiny quakes. But when the plates become locked together, this prevents any release.

The pressure builds up over a period of years until a massive quake occurs, such as the one on 18 April 1906. Although the earthquake only lasted for 40 seconds, its force (Richter Scale 8.3) was enormous. In San Francisco, 700 people died, over 28,000 buildings were ruined and over 250,000 people were left homeless.

Today, evidence of the San Andreas Fault can be seen in cracked walls and scarred landscapes (below).

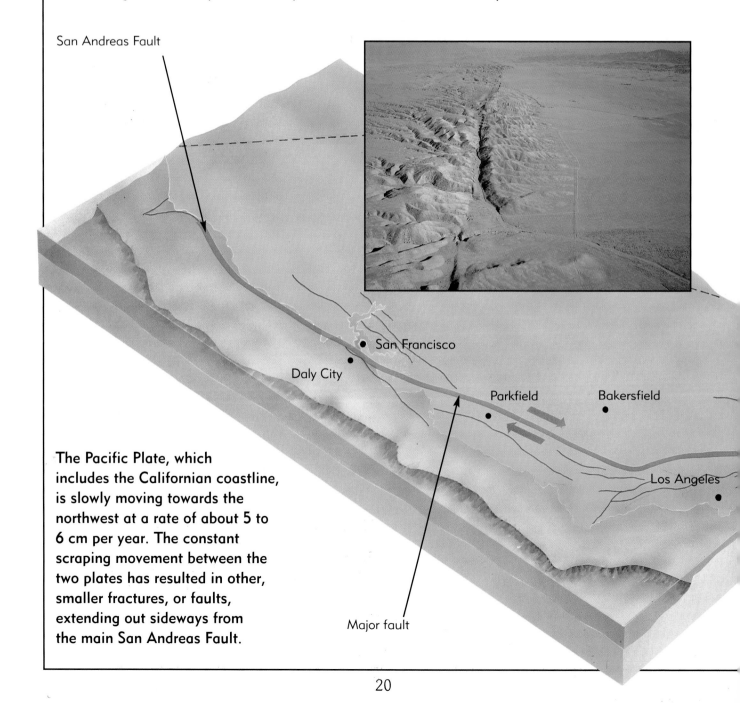

San Andreas Fault

San Francisco

Daly City

Parkfield

Bakersfield

Los Angeles

The Pacific Plate, which includes the Californian coastline, is slowly moving towards the northwest at a rate of about 5 to 6 cm per year. The constant scraping movement between the two plates has resulted in other, smaller fractures, or faults, extending out sideways from the main San Andreas Fault.

Major fault

The 1989 earthquake

A quake measuring 7.1 on the Richter Scale rocked the city of San Francisco on the 17 October 1989. Its effects were felt across an area measuring 1 million square km. The San Andreas Fault had slipped along a 40-km section, and although the initial tremor faded after about 15 seconds, a total of 6,000 aftershocks were felt. In San Francisco itself, the collapse of a concrete highway crushed 42 people to death.

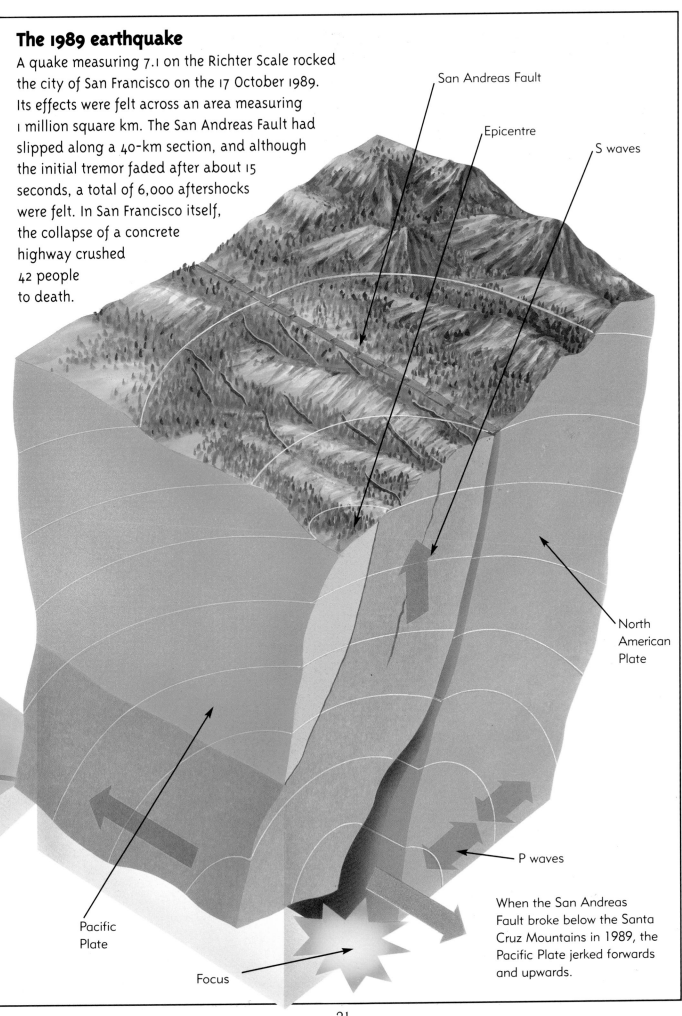

San Andreas Fault

Epicentre

S waves

North American Plate

P waves

Pacific Plate

Focus

When the San Andreas Fault broke below the Santa Cruz Mountains in 1989, the Pacific Plate jerked forwards and upwards.

EARTHQUAKES TODAY

Iran frequently experiences savage earthquakes. In 1990, a quake with a Richter scale magnitude of 7.7 struck Iran. Killing 50,000 people, and leaving 100,000 injured, it was Iran's worst ever disaster. In 1997, Iran was devastated by two further quakes. The first killed 1,000 people in the towns of Ardabil and Meshinshahr. The second killed 1,560 people and destroyed 11 villages in eastern Iran.

In 1998, a remote region of northern Afghanistan was ravaged by a 6.1-magnitude quake. It flattened 28 villages, killed 4,800 people and left thousands homeless in freezing conditions.

Several major quakes struck worldwide in 1999. In January, Colombia shook from a 6.2-magnitude quake which killed 1,200 people and affected 20 towns. In August, Turkey was torn apart by a 7.2-magnitude quake which killed 13,000 people, only to suffer two more deadly quakes in a year. 2,300 people also died in Taiwan in September, when a 7.6-magnitude quake hit the cities of Taichang and Nantou.

In 2001, two horrific quakes occurred in January. El Salvador reeled from a quake which triggered deadly mudslides, and a massive 7.9 quake rocked Gujarat State in India's worst quake for 50 years. 10,000 people died and 30,000 were injured.

➤ The Colombian quake destroyed about half of the city of Armenia. Aside from levelling thousands of homes, the quake flattened police barracks and other public buildings in the city's main square. Townspeople dug with shovels or bare hands to free survivors from the twisted metal and smashed concrete.

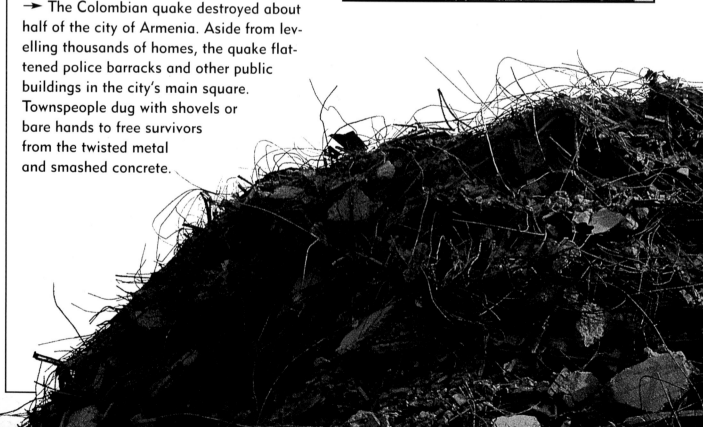

Relief efforts

The coastal town of Golçuk was hardest hit by the Turkey earthquake. Only 27% of houses here were still standing afterwards. Thousands of survivors were left homeless, and dependent on the Turkish Red Crescent — the Turkish equivalent of the Red Cross. 'Tent cities', where victims were provided with food, blankets and shelter, sprouted in the fields around Golçuk.

◄— In Bhachau, India — a small town near the quake's epicentre — over 90% of buildings were flattened. Roads, bridges and other constructions were also severely damaged.

◄—◄— In Taiwan's capital, Taipei, a 12-storey block was shaken off its foundations and smashed into a neighbouring building. Survivors of the quake watched as streets filled with water from burst water mains, and electrical fires raged through the town.

EARTHQUAKE PREDICTION

On the afternoon of 4 February 1974, a radio broadcast to the three million inhabitants of Liaoning Province in China warned them to leave their homes immediately because of an impending earthquake. Just after 7:30 that evening, an earthquake destroyed or damaged almost all of the buildings in the city of Haicheng (pop. 90,000). Miraculously, the death toll was only about 300 people. For the first time anywhere in the world, an earthquake of this strength had been predicted correctly.

Seismologists have identified several warning signs in the build-up to an earthquake: alterations in the speed of seismic waves, swellings in the ground and a large number of minor tremors along the plate boundaries. With the help of modern technology, scientists can monitor even the tiniest movement in the Earth's plates. Scientists in China have relied on a number of less scientific warning signs to predict earthquakes. They claim that, before a quake, fish become very agitated and small animals like mice and rabbits run around in panic.

→ The picture on the right shows a scientist checking the equipment installed in one of 18 water wells around the town of Parkfield in the United States. Parkfield is situated along the San Andreas Fault, an area which runs a high risk of being hit by a quake. Dozens of researchers have made the town of Parkfield the most closely monitored earthquake region in the world. Instruments in the wells record the level of groundwater as the rock beneath is affected by the build-up of pressure caused by seismic activity. The antenna situated on top of the equipment transmits data to a satellite, which then relays the information to Parkfield Experiment Headquarters for analysis.

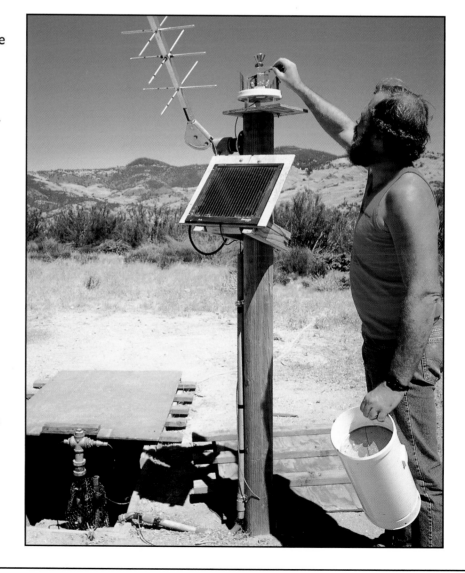

→ US monitoring stations detect movement below ground by sending lasers from one side of a fault line to a reflector on the other. Scientists measure ground movement along the fault from the amount of time it takes the beam to bounce off the reflector.

↓ A creepmeter measures movement along a fault line. A weight on the end of a piece of wire rises or falls as the fault moves.

New technology

The United States and Japan have been world leaders in developing new technology to help predict earthquakes. Scientist Ross Stein (left) has constructed a computer model of quake stress around Los Angeles. He has calculated the stresses built up by the five large area quakes since 1933, providing information on where the next quake may strike. Scientists at the California Institute of Technology are currently developing an Internet-early-warning system, which could give cities about to be hit valuable extra seconds to evacuate buildings and shut down powerlines.

TOKYO — A CITY PREPARED

Following the catastrophic effects of the 1923 earthquake in Tokyo, the Japanese saw the rebuilding of their capital city as an opportunity to plan for future earthquakes, and so avoid any further large-scale destruction.

Special regulations control the height of new buildings and the design of their internal structure. The authorities realised that they needed to protect the city's road and railway system, as well as gas and water pipes and electricity cables. To avoid the problem of a damaged water supply, making it difficult to carry out a successful fire-fighting operation, a ten-day supply of water, amounting to some 400,000 tonnes, is stored in earthquake-proof tanks in Tokyo. In addition, stockpiles of food and blankets have been prepared for the city's 8 million inhabitants.

In preparation for any future earthquake, trained disaster teams have been created, and earthquake drills are held regularly in schools, offices and factories. A constant stream of leaflets, posters and TV and radio broadcasts reminds residents about the need to be prepared. It should now be possible to give sufficient warning time, with the help of the huge bank of seismographs at the Japan Meteorological Agency.

Past earthquakes

142,000 people died in the massive earthquake (Richter Scale 8.3) which rocked Japan's Kanto Plain in 1923. Out in Sagami Bay, at the focus, the sea-bed sank 400 m. Over half a million homes were destroyed in Tokyo and Yokohama. Ironically, Tokyo's newly built Imperial Hotel was due to be officially opened that day. The hotel had been specially designed to withstand an earthquake. As the ceremony was about to begin, the quake smashed into Tokyo, bringing with it an 11-m high *tsunami*.

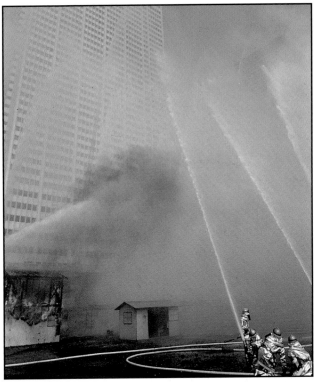

↑ The Imperial Hotel was one of the few buildings left standing after the 1923 quake. However, its design later proved to be flawed, and the hotel was demolished in 1968. The latest advances in seismic engineering were used in the design of the New Imperial Hotel (above).

↑ �le These fire-fighters in Japan are tackling a fire as part of a regular earthquake drill.

↑ Even schoolchildren are encouraged to practise earthquake drills regularly.

◄ Other earthquake-prone areas, like San Francisco (shown left), have established sophisticated emergency measures to reduce the loss of life and property during an earthquake.

WHAT CAN WE DO?

We do not yet know how to prevent earthquakes, so how can we make sure that they cause as little damage and as few deaths as possible?

Cities and towns in earthquake zones should be carefully planned and designed. Gas and water pipes and electricity cables should be well protected. In some earthquake-prone areas in the United States, electricity generators automatically shut down in the event of an earthquake, and gas pipes are closed by automatic valves. Other countries are also taking protective measures. In Iran, reinforced brick structures are replacing flat-roofed mud homes, and in Tashkent in Uzbekistan concrete buildings have replaced the brick and mud structures.

The 255-m-high Transamerica Building in San Francisco (pictured below) is a monument to the success of earthquake architecture. Its triangular framework is supported by concrete-clad steel columns which should withstand even the most severe earthquake.

Foundations
A slab of concrete, reinforced with steel rods, will support the building. The walls are reinforced by securing them to the foundations with anchor bolts.

Chimneys

Brick chimneys must be secured with special brackets. Metal ones are lighter and cause less damage.

An earthquake-resistant house should be a low structure made of reinforced concrete. There should be strong walls on the first storey, where the effects of the quake are greatest. Foundations should be deep or flexible so that the building can sway as the ground beneath it shakes during a tremor. It is better to build on solid rock such as granite. Clay, sand and other soft surfaces increase the effects of seismic waves.

Beams and joists

Extra reinforcement is essential where wall beams and floor joists join up. The house must be able to withstand both the vertical and horizontal shaking movements experienced during an earthquake.

↓ The wide streets of San Francisco help to prevent the spread of fire during an earthquake, and also allow buildings to sway, without crashing into each other.

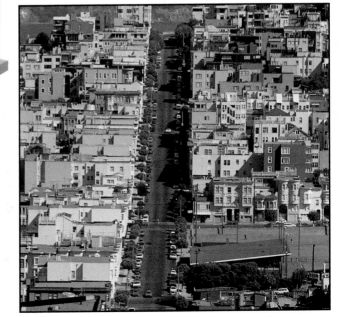

Water heater

Boilers, generators and water heaters are firmly secured to prevent them breaking loose and fracturing gas pipes.

FACT FILE

The worst death toll

The largest number of deaths from an earthquake was believed to have occurred around July 1201. The earthquake affected the Near East and eastern Mediterranean regions, leaving an estimated 1.1 million dead.

An earthquake in the Chinese city of Tangshan in 1976 measured 7.9 on the Richter Scale. The death toll was originally believed to be about 650,000, but was later reduced to 242,000 by the Chinese Government.

Largest earthquake

An earthquake measuring 8.9 on the Richter Scale struck Alaska in the United States on Good Friday, 27 March 1964. The damage caused by the quake was estimated at US $750 million. Five hours after the first tremor, a giant *tsunami* demolished the Alaskan port of Valdez, while at the oil port of Seward, a 10-m wave topped with burning oil surged across the dockside, sweeping away all the port's facilities.

Miracle survival

On 9 December 1999, 80 days after the Taiwan quake, a cat was discovered alive in a building in Taichang. After treatment it made a full recovery.

Historical patterns

Scientists cannot ignore historical patterns when predicting earthquakes in some quake-prone areas. In Mexico, where five times as many earthquakes occur each year as in California, a major earthquake occurs every 35 years. The strength of the shock waves unleashed by the 1985 quake there were 1,000 times more powerful than the atomic bomb which destroyed Hiroshima in Japan at the end of the Second World War.

In the small town of Parkfield, midway between Los Angeles and San Francisco, an earthquake occurs every 20 years. Cameras have been installed in a local bar in the town to record the event of the next earthquake. In San Francisco, scientists predict a strong possibility of a major quake occurring before the year 2020.

Most homeless

A quake which struck Guatemala in Central America in 1976, broke records for post-quake homelessness. One million people lost their homes over an area of 5,500 kilometres.

Financial loss

In January 1994, a moderate but very damaging quake struck the densely populated San Fernando Valley, near Los Angeles. In terms of financial loss, it was one of the worst natural disasters ever in the US.

Worst Russian quake

Russia experienced its worst ever quake in 1995 in the small town of Neflegorsk. A 7.5-magnitude quake flattened 16 of the town's 19 buildings.

RECENT EARTHQUAKES

1999

Turkey

(7.4 Richter Scale) A quake levelled the coastal town of Golçuk. 13,000 were killed, and many survivors lost everything.

Greece

(5.9 Richter Scale) 52 people died when the strongest quake for a century hit Athens. More than 100 buildings collapsed during the 10-second quake.

Taiwan

(7.6 Richter Scale) 2,300 people died in a quake centred in Nantou county, 150 km southwest of the capital Taipei.

2000

Indonesia

(7.9 Richter Scale) Earthquakes are common in Indonesia, which is located in the Pacific Ring of Fire. This one was fatal — 58 died and hundreds were injured.

2001

El Salvador

(7.6 Richter Scale) 872 people were killed in a quake which caused massive mudslides in San Salvador. 10% of the population were made homeless. Two further deadly aftershocks killed hundreds more.

India

(7.9 Richter Scale) Over 10,000 people died in India's worst quake for half a century.

GLOSSARY

aftershocks – extra movements of the ground which occur after the first shock waves.

crust – see lithosphere.

epicentre – the place on the Earth's surface directly above the focus of the earthquake.

fault – a weak point in the Earth's crust where the rock layers have ruptured and slipped

focus – the point inside the Earth's crust where the shock waves of an earthquake are released.

lithoshpere – the outer solid layer which surrounds the Earth. It consists of the crust and the upper mantle.

L (long) wave – a type of shock wave which travels along the surface during an earthquake and causes the most serious damage.

magma – the hot liquid rocks which lie beneath the Earth's crust.

Mercalli Scale – a system used to measure the strength of an earthquake according to the amount of damage caused and the effects felt at the time of the tremors.

oceanic ridge – a type of plate boundary where new ocean floor is created by rising magma, which cools and hardens.

plate – one of the huge sections which make up the Earth's crust. The plates are continuously moving.

plate boundary – the place where two or more plates in the Earth's crust meet. Most earthquakes occur along plate boundaries.

P (primary) wave – a type of shock wave which is released from the focus of an earthquake. P waves are the fastest type of seismic wave.

Richter Scale – a system which measures the strength of an earthquake by using information recorded by a seismograph.

Ring of Fire – a belt of volcanoes around the Pacific.

secondary tremor – violent trembling of the Earth's surface which is caused by surface, or L, waves and results in the most serious earthquake damage.

seismic wave – a huge burst of energy which is released from the rocks inside inside the Earth during an earthquake. Seismic waves are also called shock waves.

seismograph – an instrument which measures movements in the Earth's crust as wavy lines on a moving sheet of paper.

seismologist – a scientist who measures and studies shock waves to find out more about earthquakes.

shock wave – see seismic wave.

subduction zone – a type of plate boundary where part of the Earth's crust is destroyed as one plate is forced down beneath another.

S (secondary) wave – a type of shock wave which travels from the focus of the earthquake up to the surface.

transform fault – a type of plate boundary where two plates move against one another. Transform faults occur at right angles to oceanic ridges.

tremor – a violent shaking of the ground caused by the shock waves from an earthquake.

tsunami – a huge sea wave caused by an earthquake occurring on the sea-bed. *Tsunamis* can be up to 30 m high.

INDEX

Photocredits

Abbreviations: l-left, r-right, b-bottom, t-top, c-centre, m-middle

Front Cover both — Corbis Royalty Free. Back Cover — Nasa. 3, 11tr, 20, 22m, 23tr, 23m, 25ml, 25tr, 27tr. 27m, 27b, 29 — Frank Spooner Pictures. 4-5, 12l — Spectrum Colour Library. 12r, 19, 24 — Science Photo Library. 13t — Piero Pomponi/ Frank Spooner Pictures. 13b — Michael S. Yamashita/CORBIS. 15tr — Vince Streano/CORBIS. 16b — Earthquake Research Institute of the University of Tokyo. 17tl — Ancient Art and Architecture Collection. 17b, 19t — Mary Evans Picture Library. 27tl, 28 — Spectrum Colour Library. 22-23 — The Hutchison Library. 22m — Rex Features. 23ml — Erick Bonnier/Frank Spooner Pictures. 23tr — ABC Ajansi/Frank Spooner Pictures. 25bl — Roger Ressmeyer/CORBIS. 26 — Popperfoto.